T0065464

RECEIVE

Natasha E. Caravati, LPC, NCC

WESTBOW
PRESS®
A DIVISION OF THOMAS NELSON
& ZONDERVAN

This book is a work of non-fiction. Unless otherwise noted, the author and the publisher make no explicit guarantees as to the accuracy of the information contained in this book and in some cases, names of people and places have been altered to protect their privacy.

WestBow Press books may be ordered through booksellers or by contacting:

WestBow Press
A Division of Thomas Nelson & Zondervan
1663 Liberty Drive
Bloomington, IN 47403
www.westbowpress.com
844-714-3454

Because of the dynamic nature of the Internet, any web addresses or links contained in this book may have changed since publication and may no longer be valid. The views expressed in this work are solely those of the author and do not necessarily reflect the views of the publisher, and the publisher hereby disclaims any responsibility for them.

Any people depicted in stock imagery provided by Getty Images are models, and such images are being used for illustrative purposes only. Certain stock imagery © Getty Images.

ISBN: 978-1-6642-2257-1 (sc)
ISBN: 978-1-6642-2258-8 (hc)
ISBN: 978-1-6642-2256-4 (e)

Library of Congress Control Number: 2021902110

Print information available on the last page.

WestBow Press rev. date: 03/15/2021

———— ✺ ————

To all those who have poured into me over the years.
I am a better person because of you. Forever grateful
for your hands and feet that serve Jesus and by default
serve me. I could not have written this without you.

———— ✺ ————

CONTENTS

INTRODUCTION

I can't do this. I will never get this right. I am not enough. Bad things will happen to me. I am unlovable. We have all had these thoughts, but they are not helpful. When our thoughts are unhelpful, they negatively impact our emotions and our behaviors. As a licensed professional counselor, I have worked with many clients over the years to help them process areas of worry and hurt in their lives. I often see clients struggling due to their unhelpful thinking.

I fully believe our minds were created by God, for God. "For in him all things were created: things in heaven and on earth, visible and invisible, whether thrones or powers or rulers or authorities; all things have been created through Him and for Him" (Colossians 1:16 NIV). God gave us the ability to think, and with those very thoughts, we can glorify Him. "And whatever you do or say, do it as a representative of the Lord Jesus, giving thanks through Him to God the Father" (Colossians 3:17 NLT). It's biblical to think positively, but this can be hard if we are not aware or used to doing so. We can learn to become aware of our unhelpful thinking by praying over our thoughts, listening for the Lord, and recognizing thought patterns we may have that are unhelpful.

This book will describe the ten most common unhelpful thinking styles, using personal examples from my life and clients I have counseled. I have also struggled with these unhelpful ways of thinking. Through self-awareness and prayer, I have learned to manage them.

In addition, I will use examples from the Bible to help illustrate how these unhelpful thoughts are common and how the Lord interacted with those who struggled with them. Throughout the Bible, scriptures show the patience of God toward his people and desire to help them grow and live as He intended. Jesus came to give us life, and life to the fullest (John 10:10) healed, whole, free, and reflecting His glory. Jesus invites us into this freedom daily, but often our minds distort this truth.

In counseling sessions, I use a Christ-based and cognitive behavioral therapy approach to help my clients become aware of their unhelpful thinking. We work together to untwist the unhelpful thoughts and find a way to make them more positive. I help them see they are the author of their perspective, and have the ability to choose their thoughts.

In my sessions over the years with clients, I have noticed that unhelpful thinking styles are not common knowledge. There are a lot of books that explain how our thoughts affect our emotions. Few connect thought patterns to the Truth that thinking positively is something Jesus told us to do from the beginning. After listening to a sermon, I felt encouraged to write this book to help explain these unhelpful thinking styles to those who were feeling lost and hurting.

The purpose of this book is to help share how positive thinking is biblical and scientifically proven to improve your mental health and quality of life. If you are angry, mad, sad, or anxious; dealing with low self-esteem; or feeling like everything is your fault, I invite you to read this book. I hope it will help you become self-aware of your unhelpful thinking so you can hand these thoughts over to the Lord and begin to think differently. It may also aid as a resource for your small group, friends, or loved ones. Anyone has the authority to change their thought patterns through prayer and self-awareness.

As you read, you will recognize many of these unhelpful thinking styles have overlapping characteristics. Similarly, the ways to overcome them also overlap and are explained more in the last chapter of this book. This application chapter will aid in helping you make the most of this book. At the end of each chapter, you will find a prayer prompt and a short script. I encourage you to modify this prayer to fit your unhelpful thinking and your own personal story.

This book is not intended to diagnose or treat anyone. If you feel you need professional help, I pray that you reach out to a qualified individual in your area and this book will be an additional tool for you.

CHAPTER 1

LABELING: COLLEGE MAJOR

Labeling: An unhelpful thinking style where people
assign labels to themselves or others based
on a generalization or another person's comment.

The Example

I still remember where we stood when we had this conversation. We were right outside my freshmen college dorm. My sister was a fifth-year college senior, and I was one month into my first year. I started college out as a business major. Within three classes of Business 101, I knew it was not the best fit for me. I briefly mentioned to my sister I was thinking about becoming a counselor to help people and wanted to switch my major to psychology. Without missing a beat, she told me, "You can't do that. You would be miserable."

"What? Why not?" I responded.

"Because you care too much about people, and you're too emotional," she said.

I believed her. I called my mom shortly after our exchange and mentioned how my sister felt I would be too emotional to help others through counseling. My sweet mom agreed. Therefore, I labeled myself as emotional. I changed my degree to sociology in hopes to become a lawyer for an international organization that stops sex trafficking. The irony is not lost on me: I recognize this too would be an emotionally demanding job. At the time, though, I thought that I could still help those who were hurting, since I "cared too much" to help others through counseling. I doubted myself based off a quick conversation. Gratefully, God pulled me out of my thoughts and aligned me back on the path He chose for me, even if at the time I labeled myself inadequate.

CBT Counseling Theory

Situations like these seem unimportant at the time, but they have the ability to produce conflict in a person's mind. When I recall this conversation now, it seems quite humorous. At the time, lies came into my mind and gave me a narrative of self-thought that was untrue. The way our minds create these narratives can vastly impact our cognitive thoughts. For example, one person may look at this situation, ignore the label of being "emotional," and feel confident in their own beliefs. Another may take the same situation and drown in the depths of resurfacing wounds and stereotypes—hearing thoughts like

"I'm not enough" and "Something is wrong with me." Research suggests the way someone perceives a situation vastly affects the way their mind and body will react.[1]

Our thoughts have a huge effect on our emotions and thus our behaviors. This is the premise of cognitive behavioral therapy (CBT). Counselors who use CBT help their client investigate themselves and become more aware of their thoughts. CBT's goal is to focus on three areas: coping skills, cognitive restructuring, and problem solving.[2] CBT research shows that negative thoughts, either fleeting or those we dwell on, can cause a severe physical and mental reaction.[3]

Let me explain using a common example.

Imagine someone pulling out of a store's parking lot and another driver cuts him or her off. The person can think, *Wow, they obviously are a bad driver. They did that on purpose.* This thought alone will automatically instill the feeling of anger and annoyance. When our bodies are angry, we release the chemicals epinephrine and adrenaline. Our brains trigger the amygdala, the active part of the brain, which oversees our "fight-or-flight" response. Oftentimes when people are in fight-or-flight mode, they can react either by freezing up, acting out aggressively, or

---

[1] Leaf 2013, 35, 72.
[2] Henderson and Thompson 2016, 406–8.
[3] Leaf 2013, 88.

in other ways they would not if they were calm. In this scenario, because this person's unhelpful thought instilled a feeling of anger, the driver may yell, honk the horn, or mumble something mean under his or her breath. Our thoughts cause our feelings which cause our behaviors.

But what if you were to think differently? Instead, you pull out of a parking lot, and another driver cuts in front of you. This time, you think, *Wow, they must be in a hurry. I hope everyone is okay.* This thought will automatically change the chemicals being released in your body. You may feel concern, neutrality, and even compassion. Your physical being will relax or stay neutral since you did not have a spike in neurochemicals. Your behavior will follow. This person who thought more compassionately may shrug their shoulders and could even start singing along to the radio as no disaster came to them. Science is showing us how our thoughts alone can have a vast impact on our mental and physical health. [4]

CBT counselors work with their clients to identify their present problems, regardless of their diagnosis. The attention shifts to the client's past for two reasons. The first is because the client expresses a strong preference to do so in session. The second

---

[4] McCabe 2015, 179–80.

is because the client is "stuck" in their dysfunctional thinking, and understanding the roots of their beliefs can potentially help them modify these rigid and unhelpful thoughts. Cognitive behavioral therapy's focus is on restructuring these irrational thoughts. These negative thought patterns are called cognitive distortions.[5] We can think irrationally every day without even recognizing our cognitive distortion. Individual therapy can often help bring these distortions to the forefront.

In my example, where I doubted myself, I called myself emotional and inadequate. I was using the labeling distortion. I was beating myself up, labeling myself with words I would never use to describe a friend. This labeling distortion affected my body like a poison. It lowered my self-confidence, self-esteem, and held me back from a goal.

With a lot of my clients, their labeling distortions come from years of verbal abuse and self-bullying. They have been told by others and sometimes by themselves they are ugly, unworthy, unlovable, crazy, strange, fat, lazy, senseless, and gross. I witness my clients in tears over words they had applied to themselves based on years of abuse. I help clients let go of these labels, and if they cannot let go, we define them differently. For example, the word *weird* can now have a positive connotation instead of a negative one. We work together to redefine how they view these unhelpful labels.

A simple technique I use with my clients to help challenge their labeling thoughts is to imagine them saying this thought to a good friend. I ask them to role play with me. I reverse their

---

[5] Murdock 2017, 315.

statements and say the words they just spoke to me back to them. "Imagine I am your friend, and I come to you and tell you that I failed this exam in my math class, I feel like a failure, and I don't think I will ever be smart enough to pass. What would you tell me?" Often, my clients will laugh. Because they realize how much they bully themselves and then say kind words back to me. The client then says something like, "I would tell you, 'You're being too hard on yourself. You are smart! It was a hard test, and next time you will study better and earn a better grade.'" You have the ability to do this too.

Research and counseling theories are not the only things that show us the impact of negative thinking. It is not okay to label ourselves in a way that does not glorify the Lord. Scripture has been telling us this all along. The problem comes when people do not have an accurate view of God and, therefore, cannot have an accurate view of themselves.

Scripture

Scripture tells us we are children of God—thought about, cared for, meaningful, purposeful, and cherished by the Creator of the universe. Throughout the Bible, He calls His believers "perfect, and made new" (2 Corinthians 5:17 NIV), as well as "chosen, dearly loved, and a royal priesthood" (1 Peter 2:9 NIV). God "has more thoughts about you than there is sand on the seashore" (Psalm 139:18 NIV). Yet our minds can play tricks on us, and we can ignore these truths we know and label ourselves and others with lies from the enemy. The enemy is real, and the

Bible tells us we need to be alert. "Be alert and of sober mind. Your enemy the devil prowls around like a roaring lion looking for someone to devour" (1 Peter 5:8 NIV). When we are tricked, thoughts that label us seem so small, but these thoughts can fester and mold into something vastly uncontrollable. Proverbs hints at this: "As a man thinks in his heart, so is he" (Proverbs 23:7 NAS).

I do not blame my sister for her comments, nor do I hold a grudge. It was I who missed out on an opportunity to take that conversation before the Lord, asking Him what he thought of me and how He viewed me. I was the one who took a quick, three-minute conversation and applied it toward the trajectory of my life without bringing my thoughts before Jesus and others who could have provided biblical counsel or prayed over my options. In that moment, I had limited self-awareness I was even doubting, labeling, and bullying myself. Often I see this happen with the clients I am blessed to work with every day.

We see this same labeling distortion at work in Luke 7:36–50. A woman came up to Jesus and wept at His feet. She wiped her tears away with her hair and then poured a very expensive bottle of perfume on Jesus's feet. Historically, this is a sign of worship and preparation of burial, meaning this woman knew who Jesus was and believed that He was the Son of God and would die for her. But despite the love and faith this woman had in Jesus, a Pharisee (a teacher of the religious law) saw this event occur and scolded not only her but also

"The world labeled her dirty. Unlovable. Broken. Unworthy. But Jesus did not. Jesus labeled her loved."

Jesus. "When the Pharisee who had invited him saw this, he said to himself, 'If this man were a prophet, he would know what kind of woman is touching him. She's a sinner!'" (Luke 7:39 NLT). The Pharisee labeled her a promiscuous woman and a sinner. This man also told Jesus He was in the wrong to have contact with a woman like her. Jesus strongly disagreed; despite the labels this man placed on her, Jesus argued her worth, value, and forgiveness. "Therefore, I tell you, her sins, which are many, are forgiven—for she loved much. But he who is forgiven little loves little" (Luke 7:47 ESV). The world labeled her dirty, unlovable, broken, unworthy. But Jesus did not. Jesus labeled her loved. Jesus recognized her worth regardless of the labels His followers placed on her. When we choose God, our identity is forever linked to Him. We are no longer outcasts or broken; we are made new. "Therefore, if anyone is in Christ, the new creation has come. The old has gone, the new is here" (2 Corinthians 5:17 NIV).

When you label yourself outside of the words that Jesus and God define you as, those words are being spoken against the beautiful glory of God. You are the reflection of God's glory (2 Corinthians 3:18 NLT). And when you speak poorly about yourself, you are essentially beating up God's creation. Truth is not contingent on our circumstances, nor the lies others or we tell ourselves. Stop labeling yourself with lies. If God does not use those words to label you, then you need not use them to label yourself. You cannot give up your dreams or your desires to do things

"Truth is not contingent on our circumstances, nor the lies others or we tell ourselves."

based off a lie. Allow Him to heal your negative labels and change them to positive labels. I invite you to receive His help and find your identity in God.

Prayer

Ask God to show you where you are labeling yourself with lies. Ask Him to help you to see the truth about who you are and to believe it.

God, I confess that I have struggled to label myself with the truth from Your Word. I have made it about me and my inadequacies, and not focused on the truth of who You have made me to be. I thank you that because of the cross, You have made me enough, and I no longer need to dwell on negative thoughts I have about myself. Thank You, Father, for the gospel and the words that define me now. I pray that I will search how You view me first over my negative self-view. I desperately need Your help to redefine how I see myself. Amen.

❖

CHAPTER 2

JUMPING TO CONCLUSIONS: HOUSE KEYS

Jumping to Conclusions: An unhelpful thinking style
where a person predicts the future and assumes
something bad will happen, or where a person assumes
they know how another person is feeling or thinking.

The Example

The house was beautiful. It was a Victorian home that had been remodeled for a girls' group home. It contained a giant living room, a den, a dining room, and a medium-size kitchen, where the smoke alarm would go off any time a person would open the oven while cooking. Eight girls aged thirteen to eighteen occupied the four bedrooms upstairs, leaving three offices: one for the visiting therapist, one for the director of the home, and one for the regular staff who rotated in and out daily.

There were two keys, bright silver in all their glory, and they controlled the twenty-five locks within and around the home. And because it was a group home, doors to the pantry, kitchen, offices, closets, and other spaces were to be locked at all times unless staff was present. Full-time staff were privileged with their own set, and part-time workers received a spare set to share.

After spending a lot of time at the group home during my internship in graduate school, I was offered a paid part-time residential flex counselor position. My internship was unpaid, and my husband worked in ministry at the time, so I jumped on this new offer. This new position meant I would make myself available to work during busy shifts and lend an extra hand when needed. Three days after I was officially on the job, the spare keys had gone missing. Unfortunately, I was the one who recognized their absence, and because I was the one who had used them the night before, panic struck me. My heart sank even lower when I heard the staff responsible for the missing keys would have to not only pay for the locks to be replaced but would also be terminated. Not to mention if one of these girls did have the keys in their possession, she could potentially go through the home and take or destroy anything she wanted—or worse, hurt herself or one of the other girls.

CBT Counseling Theory

How does the mind perceive information like this? It races, jumps to conclusions, and denies the truth. In this case, I immediately jumped to conclusions, which paralyzed my body, mind, and soul. Anxiety washed over me like a wave. It was hard to breathe, I felt responsible, and I thought the worst. *What if a girl broke into the therapist's office and read the other girls' files? What if she stole from the office? What if she found a knife and cut herself or hurt a staff member in the house? What if I am fired from my first paid job in the counseling field and can never get a job again?* Even writing these thoughts down causes my heart to beat faster. That is the way the mind works.

Our minds tend to think about the future. I believe this is because we were created by a God who wants us to set our minds on things above, to live for our eternal future in heaven (Colossians 3:2 NIV). We can be sitting in a room, completely safe and secure, and hear a noise. Suddenly our minds can go to the worst possible conclusion—*What if someone is breaking into my home?* This thought can automatically instill the flight-or-fight response even when there is no actual threat. The mind has so much control over the body that it can relax it or cause it to panic.[6] When the mind thinks of good things, the body will begin to ease. For instance, think about a good vacation you had with your family, and your body will begin

---

[6] Bruing 2016, 13–33.

to automatically relax. The mind is powerful in its ability to control the body.

In my outpatient practice, I have noticed jumping to conclusions has been so normalized that often my clients do not recognize they are doing it. I've had clients say, "As soon as I wake up, I think the day will be bad," or, "I don't even want to get out of bed because I just know something will go wrong that day." Some claim these thoughts help prepare them in case of an emergency. But really, this way of thinking increases your anxiety because you become anxious over a threat that may never occur. Consider this: instead of saying "what if bad," what if you could learn how to say, "what if good"?

Jumping to conclusions can also cause you to assume how someone thinks about you. This is called mind reading or fortune telling. Clients might say things like, "If I ask my boss for help, she will think I am bothering her, or I don't know how to do my job." This assumption can lead to anxious thinking or can set up an environment where you feel the need to walk on eggshells and act like you know how to do it alone. You assume others will perceive you in a negative way. A subtle shift in your thoughts can radically change your relationships or environments. "What if asking my boss for help will show her that I care about my work, and I want to do a good job?"

A CBT technique that works well with jumping to conclusions is asking the client to show you the facts. I will ask the client what event triggered these feelings. I sit down with them, and we write out the feelings associated with their unhelpful thinking. Then we list out all the facts that support their unhelpful thought. After that, we list out all the facts that do not support their unhelpful thought, including any scripture that may be helpful for them. Finally, we look together at all the columns and come up with a more balanced and realistic thought after seeing all their facts together.

Situation/ triggering event	Feelings	Unhelpful thought	Facts that support unhelpful thought	Facts that do not support unhelpful thought:	More realistic and balanced perspective	Re-rate emotion
Going for a walk	Worried 80% Scared 10% Embarrassed 10%	If I walk this way, I will die.	I have people in my family who have died young: *aunt: heart attack at 40 *cousin: cancer at 32 *cousin: car accident at 43	*Jumping to conclusions *Chances of that happening are slim *It has never happened before *I can't predict the future "God is our refuge and strength, always ready to help in times of trouble" (Psalm 46:1 NLT)	I cannot predict the future, and I have a God I can lean on if anything were to happen.	Worried 10% Confident 85% Content 5%

Another example could be as follows.

Situation/ triggering event	Feelings	Unhelpful thought	Facts that support unhelpful thought	Facts that do not support unhelpful thought:	More realistic and balanced perspective	Re-rate emotion
Not understanding a work assignment	Unintelligent 45% Embarrassed 50% Scared 5%	*If I ask for help, they will think I don't know how to do my job.*	When I was ten, I asked for help, and the teacher made fun of me.	*Jumping to conclusions (mind reading) *Other teachers have helped me in the past without making fun of me *I have received positive feedback on my performance reviews for good communication *Thoughts aren't facts "Whatever you do, work at it with your whole heart, as if you are working for the Lord, not for man" (Colossians 3:23 NIV)	It's okay to ask for help, because then I will know I am doing it right and being a good steward at my job.	Worried 5% Confident 95%

Scripture

Scripture tells us to hand Jesus our anxieties, and He will take it from there. Yet we continue to wrestle in our minds, not trusting Him and jumping to the worst possible outcome. This puts our bodies in a state of perpetual pain and misery. There is a reason Paul writes in Philippians 4:8 (NIV), "Finally, brothers and sisters, whatever is true, whatever is noble, whatever is right, whatever is pure, whatever is lovely, whatever is admirable—if anything is excellent or praiseworthy—think about such things." These words were written down in our Bible because God knew we need to hear these words, and science is the one catching up. The blessing is we have an ability to choose our thoughts, and oh, what a blessing it is. When you know you have a choice, you can choose to think about the truth God gives us—He cares, He knows, and He provides what is needed.

There are plenty of examples in scripture where people jumped to conclusions and doubted that God would provide. In the Old Testament, Abraham is told by God that his offspring would be numerous as stars in the sky (Genesis 26:4 NIV). Imagine his surprise when he and his wife have difficulty becoming pregnant. Year after year, they struggled with infertility. I cannot imagine the frustration and confusion they might have experienced, hearing the Lord speak this and not be able to become pregnant. Instead of trusting God, Abraham and Sarah jumped to conclusions. They assumed Sarah must not be the answer to how he will produce offspring, so they decided to take things in their own control. Abraham and Sarah decided he should sleep with his wife's maid servant, Hagar. "So, she said to Abram, 'The Lord has kept me from having children. Go, sleep with my servant, perhaps I can build a family through her.' Abraham agreed to what Sarah said" (Genesis 16:2 NIV). After Hagar became pregnant with Abraham, Sarah became understandably very jealous and upset. Jumping to conclusions was not helpful. Soon, because of Sarah's jealousy, Hagar was mistreated, and she fled from her community. Thankfully, the

Lord was patient, and instead of becoming angry with Sarah and Abraham for not trusting Him or His timing, He forgave them and told them that Sarah would soon birth a baby. Sarah was shocked because she was considerably old, and she laughed at the Lord. But He provided, and this offspring went on to produce the lineage of Jesus (Genesis 17:18–22).

I often see myself and some of my clients as Sarah and Abraham. Forgetting to trust the Lord's promises and trying to handle it on our own. We can see in this one example how painful it was for Sarah to watch another woman carry her husband's child. Sometimes when we try to control things and jump to conclusions because of our anxieties, we can wound not only ourselves but others.

The truth is we are allowed to give Him our anxieties. Instead of jumping to the conclusion that He cannot help us, we can choose to trust that He is not surprised and is in control. And we will have peace. "Letting your sinful nature control your mind leads to death. But letting the Spirit control your mind leads to life and peace" (Romans 8:6 NLT). We need to trust God more than we fear what may happen.

"Trust God more than our fear of what may happen."

As for the keys, it turned out another staff member was the person who lost them. Even if I had been the one to lose the keys, God still would have taken care of me, and worrying about it in the meantime did nothing except hurt me. I lost so many tears dwelling on the negative and not trusting God. In times like these, if I were to examine the facts instead of my fears, I would have recognized that God has my interests at heart. Even if it did not go the way I hoped, He would still be there for me, listening and waiting to comfort me. I am thankful He is faithful even when we are not (2 Timothy 2:13).

Prayer

Ask God to help you examine the facts and lean on Him more than you lean on the fear of "what if."

Dear heavenly Father, I am thankful that the world is not a mystery to You. I confess that I have idolized a world where I am in control. I confess that I have focused on imagining the worst instead of trusting that whatever happens, You care about me and love me. God, please search my heart and help me lean more on You in the unknown and trust You more than I trust myself. Help me examine the facts of who You are and my situation. Father, I no longer want to fear "what if bad" I want to trust "God will come through." Amen.

❖

CHAPTER 3

MENTAL FILTERING: RECEIVE

Mental Filter: An unhelpful thinking style where a person uses tunnel vision and only pays attention to certain types of information while ignoring other evidence.

The Example

I was introduced to one of my favorite professors the last semester of my graduate program. He was so confident standing in front of the class that one would never know this was his first time teaching Counseling 505. He had a thick Jamaican accent, having lived in Jamaica for thirty-one years before coming to America to pursue further education. He was incredibly wise and taught students with gratitude and delight.

I was finishing the last semester of grad school and was desperate to find a supervisor for my counseling internship.

One day in class, I briefly mentioned this to him. Immediately, he offered me an opportunity to complete my requirement under his supervision. I felt relieved and was beyond ecstatic at this opportunity. Within days, I was working to have the internship site approved by my graduate school and filling out so many forms that my hand went numb.

After only one day working with him, he uttered the phrase he would continue to recite to me for the rest of the semester: "Don't place that on your life." Repeatedly, this phrase would find its way into every conversation—within counseling sessions with clients and stories he told of his parents and past. I would state what I thought were my faults, like, "I am bad at writing counseling notes."

He would reply, "Don't place that on your life."

As I became more comfortable in our friendship, I would tease him about his weaknesses. Once we were playing a board game, and I jokingly said, "You aren't very good at this game."

But quickly he replied, "I will not place that on my life. I will not receive that."

You see, I believed the lie that I was not good enough or did not have what it took. My professor had an answer to all the doubts and lies we hear every day, and it was a matter of choice. He chose what to believe and what not to receive. It is simple, really: his confidence laid in the truth of believing what Jesus said to be true. If it was not worthy to be said, and if it was not positive or based in truth, my professor simply chose not to receive it. You may argue someone who focuses only on the good things is an over-the-top, unrealistic optimist, but it truly is following God's Word to think on good things.

CBT Counseling Theory

Cognitive behavioral therapy has a psychoeducation component, which aims to teach clients to be their own counselors, and it emphasizes relapse prevention. In counseling, therapists who use CBT help clients define themselves and examine their strengths to build confidence and positive thinking. Focusing on our strengths can greatly impact our self-esteem and self-confidence. Oftentimes clients who struggle with mental filtering focus on all their faults instead of all their other successes. They will focus on one F they earned on a paper and ignore the five other A and B grades. They may hate the way their ears are shaped while ignoring all the other features they love about their body. They have selective abstraction: "I painted this entire room, but that one spot over there on the corner looks bad." They judge themselves on one minor detail instead of the whole.

When I work with clients to filter out the bad, I am not telling them to ignore the bad but to merely not dwell on it. When we are constantly focusing on the worst, it can impact our physical and mental well-being.

A helpful technique I use with clients with unhelpful thinking is called Socratic questioning. These questions cause the client to think about their thoughts and examine them in more detail. In the case of mental filtering, I might challenge them and ask, "Are you looking at the whole picture? What causes you to pinpoint your mistakes over your successes?" In the example with my professor, he encouraged me to not point out what I thought were my failures. He wanted to make sure I was not my biggest critic. Instead, he encouraged me to receive my worth in Christ. We have a choice to not constantly critique ourselves, but to receive the truth about how God sees us even through our failures and mistakes.

"We have a choice to not constantly critique ourselves and to receive the truth about how God sees us."

Scripture

Philippians 4:8 (NIV) states, "Whatever is pure, whatever is lovely, think about such things." Mental filtering is a cognitive distortion where people ignore the good and forget to "take captive every thought to make it obedient to Christ" (2 Corinthians 10:5 NIV). People shift their focus from what is true and focus in on the thoughts that clash with what God says is true.

The Israelites struggled with mental filtering, and it caused them to lose hope. In the Old Testament, the Lord led the Israelites out of oppression in Egypt and used Moses as the leader to help them cross the desert into what God called the promise land. While crossing the desert, the Lord provided again and again: rescuing them from slavery, opening the Red Sea for their escape (Exodus 14), providing food (manna, quail, water) on multiple occasions when they cried out from hunger (Exodus 17), leading them by a cloud of light (Exodus 13:21), and leading them the long way to protect them (Exodus 13:17–18). It was noticeably clear that the Lord was with them and helped them through the long journey. But it took only a day for them to forget this when Moses walked to the mountain to speak with the Lord alone and delayed his return. The Israelites quickly filtered out the ways the Lord provided. They believed the Lord had forgotten them, and decided to worship a golden calf instead (Exodus 32:1–9).

Every time I have studied this passage, I become so angry, asking myself how they could forget God so easily and begin to worship idols like gold statues. But honestly, when I sit down to think it through, I often realize how similar I am to the Israelites and trust my emotions over God's truth. These blind spots in our thinking are what

> "When we take our minds off the facts and see only what we want to see, this can easily cause us to spiral out of control."

cause so much harm. Often, we do not even realize we are hyper-focusing on one fact and ignoring the rest. The Israelites were hyper-focusing on the fact that Moses wasn't with them, and therefore they forgot all the ways the Lord provided thus far. When we take our minds off the facts, and see only what we want to see, this can easily cause us to spiral out of control.

The truth is God sees our faults and our successes, and He loves us regardless because Jesus died on the cross for us. A mentor once told me the best example of receiving what is true is when Jesus comes up out of the water at baptism; this event is recalled in Matthew 3. "As soon as Jesus was baptized, he went up out of the water. At that moment heaven was opened, and he saw the Spirit of God descending like a dove and alighting on Him. And a voice from heaven said, 'This is my Son, whom I love, with him I am well pleased'" (Matthew 3:16–17 NIV). Therefore, because of the cross, "we are heirs, heirs of God and co-heirs with Christ," and by grace we sit at the right hand of the throne with Jesus (Romans 8:17 NIV). So now we can believe that when God looks at us, He sees us through a Jesus-colored lens. We are now His son, His daughter, whom He loves and with whom He is well pleased. For we are saved through faith, God's workmanship, loved, and created in Christ Jesus to do incredible things (Ephesians 2:1-10). Receive it, accept the good things, accept the true things, and receive God's love for you. Do not place lies on your life because you've failed a time or two. You are redeemed and loved because of Jesus.

Prayer

Ask God to help you become aware of your thoughts that do not glorify Him, and create a filter to help transform them.

Dear Jesus, I thank You that because of the cross, You still see me as your child. So often I choose to focus on the negative and let it drive me away from the truth. I repent that I have made it about me and my struggles time and time again. I pray that You will help transform my thoughts and create a filter to weed out the bad and focus on all the truth around me. Guide me and grow me so that I may see my worth in You. I pray I may receive the truth that You offer us daily. Amen.

❖

CHAPTER 4

DISQUALIFYING THE POSITIVE: BAD SPELLER

Disqualifying the Positive: An unhelpful thinking style
where a person ignores the good things occurring around
them or that have been stated about them and believes
those good things do not count for varying reasons.

The Example

I used to pretend to be sick when it came time for spelling
bees at school. Repeatedly being the first one out, and on the
first word no less, takes a toll on you. My mom, however, was
never swayed by my cough or sore throat. She saw through
my act, and I would have to attend school anyway. It came
to the point where the school had me tested for hearing
problems because my spelling was so poor. They thought

maybe I could not hear the vowel sounds. This wasn't the problem; I am excellent at hearing. To be transparent, it wasn't until I got my first iPhone with spell-check that I discovered I was incorrectly spelling multiple words. Take *pizza*, for example. *Pizzia* was how I had thought it was spelled—until I was sixteen years old. It is still confusing to me how I never realized that until then.

CBT Counseling Theory

Those who struggle with mental filtering frequently struggle with disqualifying the positive. Not only do they focus on the bad, but they also ignore all the good there is going on around them. In sessions with clients, I hear statements such as, "Well that doesn't count because that's my mom. She has to say that about me."

Or they may disqualify other positives:

> It doesn't matter that I scored a goal, because I missed the two other shots.

> It doesn't matter that my husband made dinner when I got home, because the laundry still wasn't folded.

> It doesn't count that my child said no to drugs, because they were still at the party where drugs were offered.

When we focus on the thing that didn't go as well, we often disqualify the good things like they don't even count.

Science is proving when people think a certain way, their negative or positive thinking becomes routine. When they develop a consistent pattern of thought, they create habitual repetition in their brains through neurons. Continuous repetition will cause us to be stuck on a pattern of thinking this way for life, or until we untwist these thoughts,[7] thus normalizing unhelpful thinking. Humans are creatures of habit. We sit in the same seats in classes, and we have routines when we get out of bed. Give us twenty-one days, and we can develop a new habit.[8]

A big key to stopping disqualifying the positive is self-awareness that you are doing it. Once I am able to help the client identify they are disqualifying positive things in their life, I ask them to challenge the evidence they have used to make it a negative. For instance, "What makes you feel like your mom has to say that nice comment just because she is your mom?" "Do the points you scored in the game not count?" "What makes you feel like spelling has to hold you back?"

I can sit here and think, *The girl who is the worst speller is going to write a book. What a joke!* I am a bad speller. Wait, scratch that—I *struggle* with spelling. You see how words have meaning? Saying "I am" puts me in a box and makes me feel I have nothing else to offer than being a bad speller. I cannot allow myself to ignore all the other positive traits I have to offer.

---

[7] Wehrenberg 2008, 3–22.
[8] Leaf 2013, 148.

So what if I struggle with spelling? I have multiple degrees, a license in counseling, and experience working with people who struggle with cognitive distortions. I choose to not allow my spelling to hold me back any longer. I am *not* the girl who cannot spell.

So many of my clients benefit when they stop disqualifying the good in their lives and learn to not ignore the positives of their situation. Imagine how your brain would be different if your mind did not permit cognitive distortions to misrepresent the truth of the Father.

Scripture

When you disqualify the positive, you discount the sacrifice God made for you. He chose to come to earth to die for you because He felt you were worth it. Now imagine saying to Jesus, "I am sorry, Jesus. I know You said You died for me, but I don't believe You. There is no way I am good enough." Thoughts like these disqualify the positives of the cross, of the blood, the resurrection, and Jesus, "For God so loved the world that he gave his one and only Son, that whoever believes in him shall not perish but have eternal life" (John 3:16 NIV). He gave everything for us—and we disqualify it because we think we are not good enough. The Bible states God has given His people all the talents they will need (2 Peter 1:3). It is a cognitive distortion when we disqualify the grace Jesus gave us and instead dwell on our faults.

But often even when we have all we need in Jesus; we can

easily disqualify it. Peter experienced this firsthand when he walked on water. The event is recalled in Matthew 14:22–23. Jesus wanted to spend time alone praying and asked his disciples to travel by boat to the other side of the lake, where Jesus had planned to meet with them after. However, due to the wind, the boat shifted far from where Jesus was when He finished praying. Therefore, Jesus, walked on top of the lake to meet them. "When the disciples saw him walking on the lake, they were terrified. 'It's a ghost,' they said, and cried out in fear. But Jesus immediately said to them: 'Take courage! It is I. Do not be afraid'" (Matthew 14:26 NIV). Peter wanted to believe so badly and replied to Jesus, "Lord if it is you, tell me to come to you on the water" (Matthew 14:28 NIV). Jesus invited him onto the water. "Then Peter got down out of the boat, walked on the water and came toward Jesus. But when he saw the wind, he was afraid and, beginning to sink, cried out 'Lord save me!'" (Matthew 14:29–30 NIV). Even though Jesus was with him, it didn't count because Peter recognized that walking on water is normally impossible. He disqualified the grace and the goodness of the Lord and did not trust Him. "Immediately, Jesus reached out his hand and caught him. "'You of little faith,' He said. 'Why did you doubt?'" (Matthew 14:31 NIV). He doubted because he disqualified the truth of the Father and who He says He is. He doubted that God could equip him with what he needed to be able to defy the odds and walk on water.

"He disqualified the Truth that God could equip him with what he needed to be able to defy the odds and walk on water."

I cannot disqualify what scripture says about me. I am loved by God. Scripture tells me I am chosen, and I am His, "For we are God's handiwork, created in Christ Jesus to do good works, which God prepared in advance for us to do" (Ephesians 2:10 NIV). So what if we are the worst spellers in the world, if we failed a math test, or if we fell into temptation again? There is always a positive our minds cannot ignore. His believers are enough, because He made us enough. And when we dwell on this, our brains will be restored, and it will become a habit in times of trials. Receive this truth.

"Do not disqualify what scripture says about you."

Prayer

Ask Him to help you become aware of your thoughts when you disqualify the positives in your life. Ask Him to receive the truth that there is always something good to cling to.

Dear heavenly Father, You are good and powerful in all you do. I thank You for how you care for me and those I love. I come humbly before You admitting that I have so often disqualified the good that You have given, and the grace that You laid bare on the cross. I pray that You help free my mind of my unhelpful thinking and help me to shift focus on what is good, noble, and worthy. Help me to not doubt the power You offer through the Holy Spirit. I cannot do this without You. I pray my thinking will change to glorify You. Please, Father, remind me of Your grace and mercy when I doubt. Amen.

CHAPTER 5

OVERGENERALIZING: CAR KEYS

Overgeneralizing: An unhelpful thinking style
where a person sees a pattern based off one event
and applies it to a large group or large scale.

The Example

Keys and I do not get along. Just ask my husband. In college, I kept quite a busy schedule. I was actively involved in a ministry called Young Life, worked part-time at a horse farm, and juggled staying afloat attending classes, studying for exams, and seeing friends. Sometimes when I have too much on my plate, I easily become distracted and make errors.

One day I had rushed into the grocery store to grab some items I needed to survive for the week—the essentials like milk, bread, and cheese. I hurried back, loaded my car with the groceries, and shut the trunk. *Where are my car keys?* Missing. *How did I manage to lock myself out of my car? Did I shut them in the trunk as I finished putting in my groceries?* The car doors were all locked, and I began to think to myself, *This would happen to me.* I shuffled around the car, examining it and scrambling to think of a solution. I realized that my phone was also locked inside. I frantically checked my coat pocket for the third time. Still empty.

I decided that walking back into the store was my best option. I thought, *Maybe I will see someone inside or at least walk around and calm down.* Thankfully, my Young Life director's wife happened to be shopping at that exact time. She saw me and let me borrow her phone to call a locksmith. Thirty minutes later, he arrived, ready to break into my car. I informed him my keys were in the trunk, and away he went fiddling with my door and the key lever.

Upon his rescue, my trunk was opened, and I quickly began to search for my keys. No luck. *Where could they be?* I took out bags, groceries, and random things I had gathered over the years. No keys. The man suggested I look in my pockets again. I informed him I had multiple times, which was true. Lo and behold, while he stood there, I reached in and found my key. The lies rolled in: *Of course this would happen to you. Everything like this always happens to you. Nothing like this happens to other people.* I was using strong words like *nothing* and *everything. Nothing ever goes right. Everything is the worst right now.* These are nasty lies that do not build me up in any way. Even in this silly example, these lies affected me negatively, and they can affect you too if you choose to dwell on them.

CBT Counseling Theory

This cognitive distortion is called overgeneralizing. If someone is overgeneralizing, they believe that one single event defines everything. This type of cognition and language is significant because once you say something *always* happens to you, you start to see a pattern instead of just the single event. For example, if you were to think, *No one cares about me.* Your mind begins to look for a pattern and latches on to only the instances where the negative thought or emotion could be true. This unhelpful thinking style is similar to the Baader-Meinhof phenomenon, commonly known as frequency bias. It captures the tendency that when you are more aware of something, it increases how often you will notice it. If I buy a blue Jeep, I start to notice all the other blue Jeeps around me. Suddenly, blue Jeeps are everywhere, whereas before, I barely noticed them. In the same way, if I focus on my faults or the faults in others, I will begin to identify them more and more, instead of shifting my focus to the positives. This process can lead you to feel like you are alone and no one else can ever experience your pain.

When clients struggle with this thinking style, they feel like they are in a dark pit and there is minimal hope of getting out. Their minds have tricked their brains into thinking they are alone and not worthy of rescue. This pattern of thought can be debilitating because these thoughts can change your physical well-being. When your mind thinks, neurons fire, and they communicate through neurotransmitters. Different neurotransmitters are released based on your thoughts. If you have unhelpful thinking for extended periods of time, you can fire too many or not enough neurotransmitters, this can damage or impact the physical brain.[9] This is often why medications for mental illness can be useful: because they help the brain by balancing out neurotransmitters.[10]

This way of thinking greatly affects families I work with. A wife sees one picture on social media and thinks, *Everyone's family must be better than mine.* A woman walking through a grocery store struggling with infertility sees a pregnant woman and thinks, *Everyone else is able to get pregnant but me.* A spouse makes one mistake, and their thoughts influence their actions as they scream, "You always put the dishes away wrong." Oftentimes siblings will point fingers at one another and say, "He never has to help around the house. It is always me." Or spouses say, "She is always more focused on the kids than me." Sometimes clients in my office may overgeneralize their own feelings: "I will always feel bad," or, "I will never deserve to be happy." These devastating lies and unhelpful thinking patterns are locked in their minds, and they cannot gain perspective to see it another way.

Cognitive restructuring is a helpful technique I use with clients to help break this way of thinking and allow for a gray scale. I encourage them to challenge their perspective, and we

---

[9] Bruing 2018, 13–33.
[10] Wehrenberg 2008, 3–35.

work together to see how life does not have to be black and white. Just because they say he *never* helps or she *always* does this, or *nothing* good happens to them, does not make it true. I encourage clients to use words like *sometimes* and *maybe* to help them feel more positive and less angry, irritable, sad, and lonely. If I were to pray over and restructure my thoughts about my keys, I would see that things like this do not only happen to me, but that sometimes I make mistakes, and that is part of being human.

Scripture

When you think you are alone and have nothing left, or you can never be helped, you may be facing a trial. But you are not alone; Jesus sits in our mess with us. I see this truth play out when Jesus stands before a crowd who is ready to throw rocks at a woman caught in adultery. This event is recalled in John 8. Jesus happened to be teaching outside of the temple, and the scribes and Pharisees brought a woman who had been caught in adultery and placed her before Jesus. "They said to Jesus, 'Teacher, this woman has been caught in the act of adultery. Now in the Law, Moses commanded us to stone such women. So, what do you say?' This they said to test him that they might have some charge to bring against him. Jesus bent down and began to write in the sand. As they continued to ask him, he stood up and said to them, 'Let him who is without sin among you be the first to throw a stone at her'" (John 8:4–7 ESV). Not only did Jesus know the faults in this woman, but He also knew these men's faults as well. This woman probably felt there was no hope and nothing she could do; she was alone, scared, embarrassed, and ashamed. But Jesus rescued her from all this, simply by standing up to her oppressors and pointing out the cognitive distortions at the time: "Let any of you who is without sin be the first to throw a stone at her" (John 8:8 NIV). These men slowly realize they too have failed before, and they walked away from her and Jesus. Jesus then offered her forgiveness and grace (John 8:10–11). The Lord provided for her in a moment when she most likely felt nothing could save her.

In my example of losing my keys, I felt alone and embarrassed. I had beaten myself up over something so minimal and silly. I overgeneralized one mistake and applied it to every other mistake I had made before. This is not okay because God offers us grace and daily wipes the slate clean. If I sat with the Lord in that moment, I might have realized He was teaching me something, and He would provide what I needed. But instead of trusting Him, I leaned on my own understanding and bullied myself, His creation. We can get in trouble when we are listening to the wrong voice, a lie from the enemy, and base our identity on how others view us instead of God.

"We can get in trouble when we listen to thewrong voice, a lie from the enemy, and not the voice from the Father"

The truth is it won't always be this way, and we don't need to hide in our shame and worry because Jesus is coming back. Instead of thinking everything is bad, remind yourself there are some things going well. Look at the cross and the resurrection.

Hope is alive and well, and the enemy cannot win even if it seems like it at the moment.

Prayer

Ask God to open your eyes to your overgeneralizing thoughts. Ask Him to remind you that He works for the good of those who love him (Romans 8:28 NIV).

Dear Jesus, You are gracious, loving, kind, and pure. I am so thankful for Your unending love and mercy. I have struggled to remember at times that You are for me, and You care about me. I have been negative and pessimistic and applied generalizing statements on others and myself that do not glorify You. I pray God that You show me the sin in my heart and mind, so I can shift my thinking and be more at peace. I pray that You help me lean more on Your words and trust that You work all things out for those who believe in You. Amen.

❖

CHAPTER 6

ALL MY FAULT: SUPERVISOR

Personalization: An unhelpful thinking style where a person
blames themselves entirely for a situation that was not
completely their fault, or blames someone else entirely for
something that was not entirely that person's fault.

The Example

One day it will be funny. One day it won't be this painful.
That was all I could keep telling myself. I received my first
leadership position as a counselor when I was only twenty-five
years old. I didn't know much about being a supervisor. I knew
the mental health piece, the clinical documentation, and the
theoretical theories. I could list off clinical interventions to use
with clients from age six to forty-five. But I was inexperienced
in leadership. I was put in charge of supervising twelve
counselors at five different schools. I started out working
during the summer where we all came together to run a

clinical summer program for students with mental health diagnosis and behavioral problems. It is essentially placing all the kids the teachers struggle with—the ones who receive in school suspension or detention nearly every day—in one room and managing their behaviors, all while being therapeutic. The task is not easy.

Not to mention the staff I was managing happened to be older than me and close to one another. I felt like the odd ball out and desperately worked to gain their trust and understand what they were looking for in a supervisor. Two months in, however, six of my staff members had quit. Six of the twelve people I had started with handed me a letter (two resigned by email) saying essentially, "Sorry, I got another job." What do you do when you are newly hired, and 50 percent of your staff quit? You wear yourself down working two jobs, you learn extremely fast, and you blame yourself.

It's all my fault. That's what I kept saying to myself: *You said the wrong thing here. You did not do this right. You were too young, too short, too inexperienced, too this, not enough that, not the past person, and you did not fit their mindset.* The list could go on and on. I would toss and turn at night. I wondered why, who would leave next, and questioned decisions I had made in my leadership role. I felt sick and scared anytime a staff member came up to me to ask a question. I had to work overtime hours to make up for the absent employees. The exhaustion of that coupled with the blame I placed on myself for the situation caused me to feel ill. I felt I was not good enough, I could not sleep, and it affected my relationships.

Simply put, my unhelpful thoughts had a negative effect on my behaviors and my actions.

The truth is this situation was not 100 percent my fault. One staff member had planned to leave even before I was hired, and another was on the verge of being fired. The third had applied to a different job three times before she was finally offered a different position. The fourth hated the summer program, not me. The fifth wanted more money and was burned out, and the sixth ironically quit before I even had a chance to meet her. At the time, I struggled to believe these truths, and to be honest, I worry about even writing this down now. *What if they read this book? What if they contact me and tell me, "Actually, no, Tasha, it was exactly your fault I left."* The lie is so deeply rooted that it places me in fear of being transparent. This is how much our minds trick us due to cognitive distortions.

CBT Counseling Theory

In counseling, I see clients handle this unhealthy thinking style differently. Some blame other people and state, "It is all their fault, not mine." Others will believe they are 100 percent responsible for things they have no control over (e.g., their dad leaving before they were born, their mom's cancer, a shooting at the mall they were not even at). These thought patterns can consume us, stir up hatred, deny forgiveness, and hold us hostage.

A counseling technique that can help us learn to take responsibility for our actions is called a responsibility pie.

Counselors who use this technique ask the client to write down everything that may have contributed to an event. The first thing they write down is normally what they think is most to blame, followed by other contributing reasons. After they have completed their list of reasons, the client is asked to work backward and place the last reason first in the pie chart. The concept works because by the time the client reaches the first reason they identified (what they thought deserved most blame), the pie chart only has 10–15 percent left. They are able to recognize they blamed themselves or others without looking at all the facts. The hope is they start to see the lie they have been telling themselves—it was not actually all their fault; or they can learn to take responsibility—recognizing fault was more on them than their spouse, teacher, or peer.

In my example of being a supervisor, I felt I deserved all the blame. But if I were to place the facts (the reasons each employee left) on the pie chart, I would see that their quitting wasn't something for which I was solely responsible. Yes, I made mistakes in that leadership role, which caused me to learn and grow. But after working through this unhelpful thought with the Lord, I can see now that I was attempting to carry the burden of blame for a situation that had little to do with me. Regardless of where blame should be placed, this is where we all need to receive the power of forgiveness.

Research is beginning to identify how forgiveness impacts a person's physical and mental health. A study conducted by Akthar and Barlow (2016) found moderately strong evidence of improvement in mental and physical health for those who completed forgiveness therapy and were able to forgive interpersonal hurts.

Scripture

The cross offers this forgiveness in ways I cannot express on paper. The Father decided from the beginning of time to share the greatest love story with us (John 3:16). And God offered us a way to remain with Him here on earth through the Holy Spirit (John 14:15–18) He knew we would mess up time and time again, and He still wanted us. Nothing can change that, unless we do not believe God is who He says He is.

There is a particular time in the Bible where it would be easy for one of Jesus's disciples to buy into the narrative that He messed up and could never be forgiven. But Peter trusted the love that Jesus offered more. Before Jesus was arrested, Peter was adamant that he loved Jesus more, and declared he would never leave Jesus's side (Matthew 26:33). But when Jesus was arrested, Peter denied knowing Jesus three times. In John 21, Jesus has been resurrected and had returned to His disciples to continue to teach them. Here, Jesus reinstates Peter, restoring him to his previous position. Peter is offered forgiveness and a chance to be a part of something bigger than himself by sharing the gospel with other people. Peter could have bought into the narrative that he had disqualified himself when he turned his back on Jesus. Peter could say it was all his fault. He could believe that he had no right to share Jesus with others and had disappointed God and everyone else. Yet in Acts, we read of many occurrences where Peter stood up and stepped into his role in the kingdom. Peter was able to do this despite his past mistakes because he chose to believe what God said about him more than what others, himself, or the enemy said.

It is hard to wrap your mind around something as remarkable as God choosing broken, sinful people to be with Him for eternity. Whether it is 20 percent your fault or 85 percent your fault, if you are a believer, you are forgiven, loved, and chosen. And because we are forgiven, we can forgive others. "Get rid of all bitterness, rage, anger, harsh words, and slander, as well as all types of evil behavior. Instead, be kind to each other, tenderhearted, forgiving one another, just as God through Christ has forgiven you" (Ephesians 4:31–32 NLT). Even if we do make mistakes, God restores all things for His good (Romans 8:28 NIV). If 100 percent of my staff quit, Jesus would not have been surprised, or discouraged. He placed me there for a reason, and there I had to sit and learn to trust Him. I will not blame Him. I will receive Truth because it is the choice He gives me every day, to trust in His forgiving grace. It is not all your fault, and it's also not all their fault. Enjoy His grace.

Prayer

Ask Him to help you believe in His forgiveness over you, over others, or someone in particular.

Dear Lord, I thank You that You are a God of mercy and grace. I confess I have struggled with loving others well, and myself. I expect so much from myself and others that it often paralyzes me with worry and anger. I pray that You would help me to change my thoughts so that I can easily let go of pain and hurt and give it to You. I no longer desire to dwell on the anger and frustration in my heart, and I desire to dwell on Your truth. Jesus, please help me to shift my focus on what really matters: You. Amen.

CHAPTER 7

CATASTROPHIZING: NEW MOTHER

Catastrophizing: A cognitive distortion where a
person has an exaggerated or irrational thought
that blows things out of proportion.

The Example

Recently there has been a push for more research on how
the brain changes when women become pregnant. The body
certainly changes. It would only make sense the brain does too.
When you're pregnant, you forget things, you can't think well,
and your mind is scattered. Lots of people call it pregnancy brain.
But in my pregnancy, my mind changed even more postpartum.
A lot of women struggle with postpartum depression. A recent
journal article reported that there is a "Postpartum depression

prevalence of 17 percent amongst healthy mothers," and this does not include postpartum anxiety.[11] A lot of mothers struggle with postpartum anxiety too, which is often not discussed. For me, the lack of sleep, the baby crying, hormones, and having to take care of a new human life, I felt like a mess. I remember for the first two weeks after my first son was born, I would cry every night around six o'clock, right when we were sitting down for dinner. I wouldn't be able to eat because I was so anxious about him sleeping each night. My mind would rush into panic mode. I remember thinking, *What if he goes to sleep and doesn't wake up? What if he dies of SIDS?* Now, this is obviously a concern and not an unheard-of fear, but regardless of how often I was told by my doctors the rarity of that happening, it was controlling me. This fear held me tight.

Sometimes as a mother, I can jump to catastrophizing when I think about my son. *What if he gets in a car accident while I am driving?* I remember kissing him in the car seat and thinking, *What if this is the last time I kiss you?* I would have to kiss him three more times before we left the house. Still today, I find myself watching him to make sure his chest is rising and falling. In this situation, it makes sense as a new mother to be worried about your child. But my level of worry was unhealthy because it interfered with my daily functioning abilities. I struggled to eat, sleep, and think about anything but my son, and I was tearful every evening. Thankfully after a couple of weeks my hormones and thoughts settled as I prayed for strength from the Lord to carry my fear for me so I would not have to. This is not

---

[11] S. Shorey 2018, 235.

always the case for some women and their thoughts continue to consume them for months. This can lead to a diagnosis of postpartum depression.

CBT Counseling Theory

A lot of clients wrestle with this unhelpful thinking style. Often they do not realize their thoughts are the worst-case scenario and are surprised how others in their life are so naturally calm. For example, I've frequently heard, "My spouse is rarely anxious," and in the same breath they will say, "They just always assumes things will work out well." Their spouse has recognized there is no point in catastrophizing something they cannot control. Other clients dealing with catastrophic thinking might worry about going over a bridge, assuming it will collapse, or the car will crash. They will have panic attacks just thinking about their mom's doctor's appointment, assuming something horrible will happen. Some clients have mentioned fears such as, "I think if I eat solid food, I will choke and die." They catastrophize to the worst degree, and they are trapped in a web of anxiety.

When people catastrophize, they think the worst possible thing could happen. Maybe they avoid going to the grocery store, fearing, "What if a man shows up with a gun or a fire starts?" A lot of my clients say, "If I think of the worst thing that could happen, then I will be prepared if it does." Preparing is not necessarily bad, but when we overprepare by thinking of the worst possible outcome, we can negatively affect our social, mental, and daily functioning. When you overprepare, your mind is forced to think of unhelpful thoughts—what could go wrong. This more than likely will trigger the flight-or-fight response, and a rush of chemicals goes to the brain to prepare for disaster. Therefore, instead of decreasing your anxiety by preparing, your mind and body become more anxious. This is also problematic because as I mentioned before, our brains are creatures of habit and can get used to this chemical high. This can cause our minds to race to disaster for the chemical high again, even in a calm setting, essentially creating chaos out of nothing.

CBT addresses thinking and behavioral patterns. In the case of catastrophizing, the counselor can help identify irrational thoughts and replace them with rational ones. In sessions with clients, a technique I often use to combat this way of thinking is encouraging them to do reverse imagery and, or, exposure therapy. I ask my clients to shift their focus from the fearful event happening to imagining the event going well. For example, someone who is fearful of going over a bridge in their car might be imagining the bridge falling, or the car going off the bridge. I encourage them to instead imagine driving over the bridge and making it to the other side safely. I ask them to replay in their minds repeatedly their car traveling smoothly over the bridge until it becomes normal and no anxiety is felt. Once they can imagine this, I encourage them to expose themselves to the fear and drive across a bridge. This technique is called exposure therapy, and the client is now more willing and able to follow through with the task because instead of imagining things will go bad, they are better able to picture a more reasonable and less worrisome outcome. Thus, they are able to drive their car over the bridge with minimal anxiety. In the case of my son, I can use this technique as well, and instead of imagining him dying or us getting into a car accident, I imagine God holding him while he sleeps so my brain can rest. I pray over my thinking and ask God to help me imagine us getting to places safely or my son waking up from a restful sleep without any problems.

Scripture

It is okay to have big emotions. I often tell my clients, both believers and nonbelievers alike, that if we did not have any anxiety, people would run into oncoming traffic. But to those who are believers, I remind them how their emotions help them cling to the feet of Jesus to keep their souls alive. Because without these emotions, we would not be able to come humbly before the Father and recognize the need we have for Him. The point is emotions are not bad, but we cannot allow these emotions to rule our minds more than Jesus.

I will always remember a sermon where the preacher said something so powerful and profound: "You are anxious about what you idolize." In the Bible the Lord says, "Can any of you by worrying add a single hour to his life?" (Luke 12:25 NIV). And 1 Peter 5:7 (NLT) says, "Give all of your worries to God for he cares for you." I was convicted,

> **"Emotions are not bad, but we cannot allow emotions to rule our minds more than Jesus."**

recognizing my anxiety was stemming from focusing my heart more on my son than on the Lord.

Another example, when working with children who catastrophize, I read a CBT story to them about a turtle who asks *what if* questions. One question the story asks to decide whether the turtle's worry is legitimate is, "Is this an adult worry or a kid worry?" Sometimes kids worry over things that are not age-appropriate—for example, money, the car, child support, dying, or their parents' employment. I help them recognize they are the kid, and they don't have to worry about those things. It is their parent or guardian who handles those concerns. How awesome would it be for you to think the same way about your problems? What if you trusted God as your parent and believed He could handle it, and you do not have to worry about it? "That is why I tell you not to worry about everyday life—whether you have enough food and drink, or enough clothes to wear. Isn't life more than food, and your body more than clothing? Look at the birds. They don't plant or harvest or store food in barns, for your heavenly Father feeds them. And aren't you far more valuable to him than they are?" (Matthew 6:25–26 NLT).

To emphasize the point even more, while I was in undergrad, there was a quote on my wall that read, "Don't lose hope on day two." This was in reference to the feeling that many of Jesus's disciples had after Jesus died on the cross. They were lost, confused, and heartbroken. Their King was gone, and as they walked along the road to Emmaus, I can imagine their minds spinning, not sure what to think. I'm certain they were perplexed and imagined the worst: a world without their Savior. But on the third day the Lord met them on the road and spoke to them, and finally they were able to see Jesus alive again. They immediately left to tell the other disciples (Luke 24:13–35). "It is true! The Lord has risen and has appeared to Simon" (Luke 24:34 NIV). A mentor of mine once told me that catastrophizing is anticipating a future without God in it. But because of the resurrection, Jesus is alive, and therefore there can never be a future without God in it. We don't need to worry about *what if* bad, because nothing can conquer what has already been: Jesus beating death and rising again!

Prayerfully give your worries to the Lord and allow Him to manage the worry for you. Your mind will learn to surrender the worry easier each time you do this and begin to heal.[12] We must receive the truth from God, not doubting the strength He has. "But let him ask in faith, with no doubting, for the one who doubts is like a wave of the sea that is driven and tossed by the wind" (James 1:6 ESV). We are anxious about things we idolize, and if we idolize worldly things, our thoughts will likely spiral and catastrophize to the worst possible outcome. But if we idolize the Lord, we can trust He is in control and He will do what He says. We will also know we were not made for this world but eternal life with Him.

---

[12] Leaf 2013, 61–68.

Prayer

Ask Him to show you what you may be idolizing, and change your thoughts to focus more on Him. Ask God to help you lay down your burdens at His feet.

Jesus, You know my heart, and I am so thankful for that. I ask for forgiveness in the things I have been idolizing. Often, my mind is wound up in anxious thoughts, and I know this is because I am putting these things before my trust in You. I pray for You to help me change my thoughts and renew them daily to focus more on You. I lay down my worries and anxieties and ask that You mend them and hold on to them for me so I no longer have to carry their weight. I no longer want to lose hope on day two. I greatly need You, Father, and am so thankful for Your grace. I believe there is no such thing as a future without You in it. Amen.

CHAPTER 8

SHOULD AND MUST: SETTING THE BAR

Should and Must: An unhelpful thought
where a person uses critical words to define
expectations, their self or someone else.

The Example

Now I am going to be calling out all my perfectionist, type-A personality, black-and-white, no-room-for-error, sometimes procrastinator friends, because this chapter is for you and for me. The "perfect mom," "perfect spouse," "nicest person," "has it all together all the time," "I should be this way," "I must do it right," "he must do it this way," and "she should know better." This cognitive distortion is sneaky, and it places expectations on people, including ourselves, that are unfair, unbiblical, and flat-out soul-crushing to whoever is involved. Marriages and friendships break apart because of this unhelpful thought scheme. People don't ask for help because they feel they should have it all together on their own. Or they weigh themselves down by unrealistic standards they place on themselves because they constantly feel like they should be doing more. This way of thinking is exhausting and devastating to our minds and hearts.

One example of this is when I place unfair expectations on others, especially my Christian friends. It's hard for me to give grace to those who know Jesus because I think, *They should know better. They must know better.* My spouse must love me this way because he should know that's what makes me most happy. My friend should call me once a week instead of me constantly being the one reaching out to her because that's fair. She should have known better to not raise her voice that way because she knows Jesus. This thought process becomes even more aggressive when we place this distortion on God. For example, have you ever said, "God should and must answer my prayer"? Or do you know others who have said something like, "God must show up. God should be helping, doing something ..." When we place these expectations on others and ourselves, we set ourselves up for emotional hurt, strained relationships, and lost friendships. When we place these expectations on God, we set ourselves up to doubt Him and His goodness.

CBT Counseling Theory

In marriage and premarital counseling, one of the biggest struggles I have seen with couples is their expectations. The couple comes in, pointing fingers and yelling at one another because they have placed expectations over the other (most of the time without even verbalizing it). A wife may assume the husband is to be home at a certain time, and the husband may assume the wife should be doing things around the house without communicating these thoughts. Or the wife may say, "He should be more empathetic with the kids," and the husband might respond, "Well she shouldn't baby them so much." Being self-aware that we place pressure on ourselves or other people can help us avoid frustration. When we think more flexible and positive thoughts toward one another and ourselves, we can begin to feel happier and healthier.

In CBT, psychological health means placing primary importance on monitoring maladaptive cognitive processes (automatic thoughts, intermediate beliefs, and schema) and testing their validity, while refining behavior with the aid of proper coping mechanisms. The bonus of CBT is that all three components (thoughts, feelings, behaviors) support one another. The counselor can break into the cycle at any point and address a thought, a feeling, or a behavior.

When clients come in with *should* and *must* thinking, I use a technique referred to as guided discovery. This method helps clients determine where these assumptions that they should or must be a certain way came from. Some discover they have memories of their childhood that lead to this rigid thinking style. They realize they have been setting high expectations that are not obtainable for most of their life. This sets them up for frequent feelings of inadequacy. I challenge them using a metaphor of a ladder: "What causes you to require your success to be at the very top of the ladder, when you say everyone else has reached success three steps lower?" This analogy helps the client realize the pressure they are placing on themselves or others. Over time, I continue reminding them of this metaphor to help them let go of their perfectionist thinking towards themselves and others.

Scripture

Scripture tells us to expect nothing: "Love your enemies, and do good, and lend, *expecting nothing* in return and your reward will be great and you will be sons of the Most High, for he is kind to the ungrateful and the evil" (Luke 6:35 ESV). God provides common grace to those who are evil and ungrateful (Psalm 145:9), so we are called to do so too, even if we think they should have done it this way instead. The Bible is clear: we are "all sinners and fall short of the glory of God" (Romans 3:23 NIV). This means not one of us will ever achieve perfection. We are never going to be perfect, and we need to stop placing this must-be attitude on ourselves and those around us.

Consider the story of Martha and Mary. Jesus had come to town, and Martha welcomed him and his disciples into her home. While Martha was working hard to prepare for her guests, Mary, her sister, sat and listened at Jesus's feet. Martha was furious because Mary was not helping. I believe this emotion deeply stemmed from Martha's should and must unhelpful thinking style. I imagine she thought to herself, *Mary should be helping me. Mary must have something better to do than to just sit there!* Martha struggled to think the best in her sister and even called her out in front of Jesus: "Lord, don't you care that my sister has left me to do the work by myself? Tell her to help me!" (Luke 10:40 NIV). These expectations robbed

> "Expectations can rob you of the joy and fullness of life Jesus offers you."

Martha of the joy and fullness of life Jesus was offering her. Upon seeing this, Jesus responded, "Martha, Martha, you are worried and upset about many things, but few things are needed—or indeed only one, Mary has chosen the better, and it will not be taken away from her" (Luke 10:38–40 NIV).

How often have we used these critical words to wound us or others, thinking we knew best when maybe we were focused on the wrong things? Many times, I see my clients call themselves out like Martha did, feeling like they should be doing more. They are their biggest critics, and when they get it wrong, they think less of themselves. But that is where the confusion comes in. God isn't calling us to bully His creation. He's asking us to think less *about* ourselves, not less *of* ourselves.

> "He's asking us to think less about ourselves, not less of ourselves"

The truth is God's grace is abounding. "Your righteous deeds are like filthy rags" (Isaiah 64:6 NIV). Live forgivingly, not only to others but also yourself. "Instead, be kind to each other, tenderhearted, forgiving one another, just as God through Christ has forgiven you" (Ephesians 4:32 NLT). If God can forgive you, you can forgive yourself and one another. Stop holding your guilt and pain, and hand it over to Him. Receive grace, not destructive criticism.

Prayer

Ask God to help you find your worth in Jesus, not in your or others' ability to do things.

Jesus, I confess that I have strived to find my worth in my ability to do things instead of You. Constantly, I feel like my worth is tied to my actions and actions of those around me instead of how You view me. Please, Father, help me when I miss this truth, and remind me of the times I do this and focus more on myself instead of You. Thank You for reminding me that I am loved solely because I was made by You. Jesus, You make me enough because of the cross, and I am forever grateful. Amen.

CHAPTER 9

EMOTIONAL REASONING: LIVING FAR APART

Emotional Reasoning: An unhelpful thinking style where a person relies on their feelings over facts or evidence. They assume because they feel a certain way, it must be fact.

The Example

I thought about leaving this lie out because it was so crippling to me. This lie came out of old wounds and caused me to connect my worth to how I thought someone felt about me and not how Jesus views me. After being married for about a year, my husband was transitioning jobs while I worked on my residency for my license in professional counseling. Residency for counselors is a little different than doctors; each state has its own requirements and counseling boards. I was a few months into my new job as a family and children's counselor at a community service board when my husband was gifted with an amazing opportunity. When I came home that night, he told me about a fellowship opportunity offered to him by someone he connected with at a conference a few years back. This nonprofit was a dream of my husband's. It helped people in the poorest places start and maintain sustainable businesses with their own community leadership. The only problem was this six-month fellowship opportunity was based out of St. Louis, Missouri. Meanwhile, my residency was in Virginia.

This was not just a long commute. It would require us to live apart after almost eleven months of learning to live together in our young marriage. I was so conflicted. I wanted the best for my spouse, and his dreams were my dreams. I only wished he was able to live with me to accomplish them. After lots of prayer and talking it through, I told my husband he should go because I knew he needed the experience, and I would regret it if I was the one to hold him back from this opportunity. A few days later, lies began to spin out of control in my mind, and wounds resurfaced I did not realize had never healed.

I started to believe my husband did not choose me and chose a career path over me. My thoughts became more focused on how my spouse felt about me than what the Lord felt about me. In my sinful thinking, I felt unchosen, unloved, and undesired because I was focusing more on my feelings about my husband than on how the Lord felt about me. Lies spun out of control and began to fester. These thoughts impacted me greatly, and him.

Our relationship suffered because of my unhealthy thinking.

I became physically overwhelmed by comparing my worth to other marriages and relationships around me. Even though I was the one who told him to go, I wondered, *Why did my husband leave to live somewhere else, but other husbands do not?* The lies snowballed, and anxiousness settled in. He felt it too. He became overwhelmed and anxious about hanging out or talking on the phone due to worrying about fighting. Because I was always on edge, he had to be as well. I chose to believe my emotions over facts. I chose to receive the lie that there must be something wrong with me. I chose to believe the lie that he did not care about me. I chose to believe the lie that I was foolish. And because I allowed these thoughts to dwell in my mind instead of thinking the best in him. I was unable to realize he had the best intentions in mind long term for our family, and our relationship suffered.

CBT Counseling Theory

Emotional reasoning is a cognitive process where an individual believes their emotional reaction proves something is true, regardless of the observed data. This is possibly the highest form of self-sabotage for clients. They trust their emotions over facts. Sometimes I have clients whose unhelpful thinking style is so strong in emotional reasoning that they have trouble breaking out of this lie, just like I did in my example.

You feel lonely, so you decide no one must care about you. You feel like you are overweight, even though your BMI is healthy and no one has ever mentioned those words to you.

Clients say out loud, "I am not worthy enough to be happy." They disqualify their ability to be happy based on a feeling! Their thoughts are assumptions. They say, "I feel unworthy, and therefore I am. I feel forgotten, unloved, and not enough, so that must be the case." It is simply not true, especially for those who have trusted in the Lord. When the brain thinks these thoughts day after day, a person's self-confidence is affected.

Good interventions to use when a client is dealing with this unhelpful thought is the CBT chart explained in chapter two, and the role play explained in chapter one. Another helpful technique I use for my younger clients who struggle with emotional reasoning is bibliotherapy, a therapeutic reading resource. I read a book to my young clients that tells all about a little monster who lives inside of their heads and how he is determined to make them feel bad about themselves. The book teaches children the monster feeds off mean lies they hear in their head. It tells them to not feed the monster by not listening to his lies. If they do not listen to the mean lies their monster tells them, he has no food to eat, and he will get smaller and smaller. As the monster becomes smaller, their self-esteem and self-confidence become bigger. I try to encourage my adult clients to do this as well, helping them see that as they listen to their emotions over facts, they can self-sabotage their happiness and the goodness God offers them. When I was believing that my husband cared more about his career than me, I was listening to distorted words and feeding the enemy, allowing him a foothold to intervene in our marriage.

Scripture

At the end of the day, emotional reasoning bleeds into disqualifying the positive and filtering out all the truth God offers us. It was emotional reasoning that had Moses doubt his ability to help his people—even after God talked to him personally! In Exodus 3–4, God asks Moses to speak to the Israelites and tell them His promise is going to come true, and He will bring them out of Egypt. In this conversation, God also reassures Moses on many occasions: "I will be with you" (Exodus 3:12). "They will listen to you" (Exodus 3:18). "But Moses protested to God, 'Who am I to appear before Pharaoh? Who am I to lead the people of Israel out of Egypt?'" (Exodus 3:11 NLT). Therefore, God, gives Moses the ability to turn his staff into a snake simply by throwing it on the ground! Still Moses protests, "O Lord, I have never been an eloquent [speaker], never in the past nor since you have spoken to your servant. I am slow of speech and tongue." So God reminds Moses it was He who gave Moses the ability to speak, and He will tell him what to say (Exodus 4:10-13 NIV). Regardless of all this, Moses still feels he is not enough, insufficient, and inadequate. Moses self-sabotaged himself even after all the Lord's reassurance and promises, and he pleaded to God to send someone else. The Lord, although upset, agreed that Moses could ask for help from his brother (Exodus 4:14-17). In the end, Moses passed up an opportunity to glorify God because Moses felt he was unworthy. That is heartbreaking to me.

We can choose to talk to ourselves like we talk to a friend, or we can choose to be our own worst enemy. If the roles were reversed and a friend of Moses had been asked by God instead to speak to the Israelites, Moses would have likely encouraged his friend to trust God and believe he was enough because God had chosen him. Moses, however, chose to be his worst enemy, neglected to talk to himself like a friend, and failed to trust God. We have a choice. That is the gift God offers us—we can choose to trust He has given us a love we do not deserve.

In college, my Young Life teammate Katie had a great response to such lies and often said, "I am working on choosing truth over emotion." She recognized that just because she felt like God wasn't there did not mean that was true. She wanted to fixate on the truth, not just her feelings. When we accept God into our lives, He says nothing in all creation can keep Him away from us. "No power in the sky above or in the earth below—indeed, nothing in all creation will ever be able to separate us from the love of God that is revealed in Christ Jesus our Lord" (Romans 8:39 NLT). So even in the darkness, just because we feel He isn't there and we are alone, that does not mean it is the truth. Emotions help grab our attention when we are in need, but they are not absolute truth. Thoughts are not

"Choose truth over emotion." fact. The truth is He won't leave us, so what can mere man do to harm us (Hebrews 13:5–7 NLT)? Examine and take captive your thoughts; find the facts. Emotions have power, but only as much power as you give them.

Prayer

Ask the Lord to help you see truth over emotion and believe what He says over what you feel.

Lord, I am thankful You love me despite my sin. I often feel like I am alone, unworthy, not enough, or unfit. I pray that my emotions no longer allow me to cast doubt on my ability to glorify You, or doubt the truth of Your gospel and who You say You are. I need Your help Lord in focusing on Your truth more than I focus on my feelings. Jesus, thank You for opening my heart to examine the facts and focus on You. Amen.

CHAPTER 10

ALL OR NOTHING: BOOK WRITING

All or Nothing Thinking: An unhelpful thinking style where a person thinks in two different extremes, all black or all white. The person lacks a balance in their thinking scale; they are either a failure or perfect.

The Example

If you think you are your biggest critic, try writing a book. It is interesting writing a book: each sentence is broken down, and every comma is scrutinized. You start to over analyze yourself. Reading two words turns into a debate in your head, to a downright pity party, and then to no hope at all. I would think to myself, *Does this sound right? You're using too many thats. No one is going to read this. Why are you even trying?*

A book cannot help anyone. You should not even try. This cognitive distortion is referred to as all-or-nothing thinking. An unhelpful thinking style where if you cannot do something perfect, then you should not even try. It leaves no room for error and no gray space. A lot of people might refer to this as black-and-white thinking. Another way you may have heard it before is the infamous saying, "It's my way or the highway." It is all this or nothing.

CBT Counseling Theory

People become trapped in this style of thinking. They can go one of two ways: perfectionists or procrastinators.

> Perfectionists will scrutinize every move they make. They will work hard, check all the right boxes, reread every direction, listen to every rule, and accept no in-betweens or exceptions—ever. They are inflexible, rigid, and hard to negotiate with. They will never be willing to examine a different perspective.
>
> Procrastinators, on the other hand, are only hindered by their thoughts. They would rather not try than try and fail. They struggle to accept a setback, and they would rather lose than enter competition. They are comfortable with one way and would rather get an F on a test than study because they feel if they study,

they will still get an F. They hold themselves back because of a lie—an unhelpful thought that affects their brains, which affects their emotions and therefore their behavior.

In sessions, a CBT technique that helps with black-and-white thinking is encouraging the client to reframe their thoughts. Reframing is a way to help clients look at a situation in a new perspective. I challenge my clients to see if they can find a middle ground, or a compromise for their thoughts. Instead of thinking the worst or the best, I ask them, "Could there be an in-between?" In the example of writing this book, by taking a perfectionist approach, I can think that if I do write a book but it does not help anyone, then I am a failure. On the other hand, as a procrastinator, if I think writing this book cannot help anyone and is a waste of time, I will sit on my couch and watch Netflix instead. I avoid because I do not believe I can do it perfectly. In both scenarios, I lose. In both scenarios, my negative thoughts take a toll, hindering my ability and causing me anxiety and frustration. Black-and-white thinking ignores the gray or middle thinking. By looking at writing a book with a reframed thought, I could see that the act of writing it alone would be a success, and it helped me become a better version of myself. This thought now produces a new feeling, one of confidence and betterment.

Scripture

When I think of black-and-white thinking, I think of King David. One day, David was walking around his palace and happened to see a beautiful woman named Bathsheba bathing. Although she was married to a different man in David's military, David asked that she be brought to him. The affair caused a pregnancy, and once David found out, he stopped thinking clearly. He immediately tried to cover his tracks by inviting the woman's husband to come home early from the war. His hopes were Uriah, the man's wife would sleep with her and cover David's tracks. However, Uriah was loyal to David and his army, and he refused to see his wife and enjoy any comforts while the army was in war and uncomfortable. David even tried to persuade him to go home to his wife by getting him drunk, but he still refused to see her. David panicked: either Uriah had to go home to impregnate his wife, or he had to die. There was no other option. Therefore, instead of confessing his sin to the Lord or to Uriah, David sent Uriah to the front lines of the battlefield in hopes he would be killed (2 Samuel 11:1–24). "When Uriah's wife heard that her husband was dead, she mourned for him. After the time of mourning was over, David had her brought to his house, and she became his wife, and bore him a son. But the thing David had done displeased the Lord" (2 Samuel 11:26–17 NIV). David was so fixated on acting perfectly that he could only think in two different lenses. He displayed black-and-white thinking when he assumed that if he was not perfect, then he had failed.

But the Lord was aware of this the whole time, and these acts were not hidden from His eyes. If David would have confessed his adultery and his failure, a man's life could have been spared. But David listened to the lies, he believed that he could fix his mistake on his own. David acted as a perfectionist, forgetting the grace that God has to offer.

The truth from scripture states God is our maker, and He has made you well (Psalm 139). It is okay to fail because God does not see you as a failure, and He will lift you back up (Psalm 40:2–3). It is okay to get it wrong because you are made right with Him (Romans 3:22–26). It is okay for you to try to write a book; God has placed this dream before you, and He will use whatever you produce (Romans 8:28). Do not let people look down on you because God has made you new, without fault (1 Timothy 4:12; 2 Corinthians 5:7).

God uses the little guys to do the big things (Acts 4:13). It is not just the people who have earned straight As or the people who think they know it all. Let God transform and renew your thoughts. "Don't copy the behavior and customs of this world, but let God transform you into a new person by changing the way you think. Then you will learn to know God's will for you, which is good and pleasing and perfect" (Romans 12:2 NLT). Write the book, and do not give up because you are fearful that you cannot do it perfectly. Take the risk, but rest when you need to, find the balance, the shades between black-and-white thinking.

Receive the gift Jesus laid down at your feet when He died on the cross for you. You are chosen. You have a choice. All you need to do is simply lay down the cognitive distortions and the lies from the enemy. "Do not give the devil a foothold" (Ephesians 4:27 NIV). Recognize truth was twisted when the fall occurred (Genesis 3). If you haven't yet, I pray you will accept the truth that you are loved, given grace, and redeemed because Jesus came, died for you, and rose from the grave. Receive this Truth.

Prayer

Ask God to show you Himself in a way you haven't experienced before, with a balanced mindset and a new way of thinking that offers peace.

Dear heavenly Father, thank You for listening to my prayers. I confess that I have listened more to the lies than to Your words. I confess that I often have allowed sin to play in my mind when I doubt the truth of who I am because of Your love and death on the cross. I need Your help to think better and to experience You in a way I haven't before. I pray for peace over my thinking. I pray for You to help me view myself the way that You view me. Amen.

CHAPTER 11

APPLICATION

There is a joke in my house that I don't know how to follow directions. It's partly because I don't like to follow directions (mainly when I cook). I blame my mom because she always said, "The best cooks are those who don't need recipes." So, I learned to cook without following recipes. I know how to follow a recipe; I simply choose not to. However, there are some directions that make life a little easier. For example, directions to help you build something—like the toy kitchen that comes in 189 pieces and that you have to put together because you are now Santa Claus, and no one sells anything preassembled anymore. I remember sitting down with my husband, studying these directions, and laughing at the steps and how complicated they were. It took me an hour and a half to put this thing together, and I'm proud to say I had only one screw left over. I am still not sure where that one goes, but that's okay. I'm not going to disqualify the positive. The kitchen set is built, and it looks awesome. Go me!

So how do we take these unhelpful thinking styles and apply them? What are the directions and the steps to help us think better? The purpose of this book is to help you become more self-aware of your thoughts and begin to identify the distortions. Knowing we are human and cannot do anything without the support of the Lord, we need to ask for His wisdom. Moses, David, Solomon, prophets, and even Jesus are known for doing this. Daily, they asked the Lord for wisdom and guidance. We too can do this. "If you need wisdom, ask our generous God, and he will give it to you. He will not rebuke you for asking" (James 1:5 NLT). We can try and try on our own to think positive and stop the unhelpful thoughts, but we will fail. In Psalm 119, David states because he loves the Lord, he desires to follow His decrees. As you trust the Lord and fall more in love with Him, you will begin to see your unhelpful thinking is not glorifying to the Lord. Allow Him to help you untwist your thinking. Allow Him to transform your thoughts, renew your mind, and receive the goodness He offers and the newness of life daily!

We see this truth in Isaiah 61 and Luke 4:18–19. Jesus says His purpose is to set captives free, proclaim release for prisoners, bind up the brokenhearted, and tell people they could receive God's love and forgiveness. So many of these thinking patterns hold us captive, and we are prisoners to them. But God does not desire this for us; He wants us to be free and able to fully reflect Him. Jesus lived that out. Jesus was able to separate Himself from the expectations and the negative thinking patterns of the crowds, His family, and the disciples. His relationship with the Father freed Him from the pressure of those around Him and negative thoughts. He was not afraid to live out His own unique life and mission, regardless of other people's agendas. Jesus offers us rest. "Are you tired? Worn out? Burned out on religion? Come to me. Get away with me and you'll recover your life. I'll show you how to take a real rest. Walk with me and work with me, watch how I do it. Learn the unforced rhythms of grace. I won't lay anything heavy or ill-fitting on you. Keep company with me and you'll learn to live freely and lightly" (Matthew 11:28–30 MSG).

Most importantly, remember to receive grace from Him when you stumble back into your old patterns of thinking. A lot of my clients struggle with beating themselves up over this. I like to remind them they have been thinking negatively for years before coming to see me. It's only natural their negative thoughts will take a while to untwist. Paul writes in his letter to the Romans, "I don't really understand myself, for I want to do what is right, but I don't do it. Instead, I do what I hate" (Romans 7:15 NLT). We are human, and we will have slip-ups in our thoughts. Give yourself grace when the old patterns resurface in the same way the Lord grants you grace and mercy daily. The idea is not to be a perfect positive thinker; the directions aren't written that way. The directions say, "Trust Me, let Me in, and receive Me, and I will care for you because I am God."

When you are feeling anxious, angry, sad, defeated, or any big emotion, or when you feel like you have low self-esteem, examine what thoughts are running through your mind. Challenge those thoughts and ask yourself, *What am I thinking about? Is this thought glorifying to the Lord? What is helpful about this thought? Am I trusting the Lord by thinking this way? God, help me transform my thoughts to help me trust You more.* Truly examine the facts. Could there be another way of thinking? Would you tell a friend this thought if they were in this same situation? Are you holding your thoughts captive and analyzing them? Could you be overthinking and dwelling more than you need to?

Often my clients sit in their sorrows and worries too long. I encourage them to set time limits. I use this technique a lot myself. I will give myself five minutes to feel my concerns and worries, and then I will tell myself, "I have given it the time it needs. Now I cannot think about it anymore." I hand it over to the Lord so my mind can rest. If you need longer than five minutes, that is fine too; increase it to thirty minutes or an hour. The goal is not to dwell on your anger or worries all day long.

It's also important when you think negatively that you don't try to fight it off alone. Often when clients do this, their worries and negative thoughts increase. Accept that you sin, accept your struggle with your thoughts, and hand them over to Jesus. Repent of those unhelpful thoughts. Open your hands up and be honest. "Jesus, I am struggling with jumping to conclusions. I think bad things are going to happen all the time. Can You please help me think good things are coming instead of constantly thinking bad things will come?" "Keep on asking, and you will receive what you ask for. Keep on seeking, and you will find. Keep on knocking, and the door will be opened to you" (Matthew 7:7 NLT).

If you feel as though you need further support with these unhelpful thinking patterns, I pray you will reach out to a local licensed counselor. Most licensed counselors are trained in CBT to help people recognize the blind spots in their lives and untwist their thinking. A licensed counselor can work with you to determine whether you may also benefit from medication to help you with your thinking. Sometimes medication alongside counseling can be very effective. Common grace allows us to have medication that can help in our healing on this side of heaven. God is the ultimate Counselor, but He can use His people to help guide us and mold us. Receive His grace.

My prayer is that this book has illuminated unhelpful thought patterns for you, so you can now pray over them and receive healing.

REFERENCES

Akthar and Barlow. 2016. "Forgiveness Therapy for the Promotion of Mental Health Well-Being: A Systematic Review and Meta-Analysis." https://journals.sagepub.com/doi/full/10.1177/1524838016637079.

Bruing, L. 2016. *The Science of Positivity. Stop Negative Thought Patterns by Changing Your Brain Chemistry.* Avon, MA: Simon and Schuster

Henderson, D. A., and C. L. Thompson. 2016. *Counseling Children,* 9th ed. Boston: Cengage.

Leaf, C. 2013. *Switch on Your Brain: The Key to Peak Happiness, Thinking, and Health.* New York: Baker.

McCabe, R., and I. Milosevic. 2015. *Phobias: The Psychology of Irrational Fear.* Santa Barbra, CA: Greenwood.

Murdock, N. L. 2017. *Theories of Counseling and Psychotherapy: A Case Approach,* 4th ed. Upper Saddle Creek, NJ: Pearson Custom.

Shorey, S., C. Chee, E. Ng, Y. H. Chan, W. W. S. Tam, and Y. S. Chong. 2018. "Prevalence and Incidence of Postpartum Depression among Healthy Mothers: A Systematic Review and Meta-Analysis." *Journal of Psychiatric Research* 104:235–248. doi: 10.1016/j.jpsychires.2018.08.001a.

Wehrenberg, M. 2008. "Medication Controls the Brain, but It Doesn't Tell It How to Think." *The 10 Best-Ever Anxiety Management Techniques: Understanding How Your Brain Makes You Anxious and What You Can Do to Change It,* 2nd ed. New York: W. W. Norton.

Printed in the United States
by Baker & Taylor Publisher Services

Printed in the United States
by Baker & Taylor Publisher Services